Whaling Days *in* Old Hawai'i

Maxine Mrantz

Mutual Publishing

Background images on pg. 1 and 2 by rawpixel.com on Freepik

ISBN: 978-1-949307-63-4

First Printing, August 2024

Mutual Publishing, LLC
1215 Center Street, Suite 210
Honolulu, Hawaii 96816
Ph: 808-732-1709
Fax: 808-734-4094
email: info@mutualpublishing.com
www.mutualpublishing.com

Printed in South Korea

CONTENTS

ACKNOWLEDGMENTS

My thanks go to the Hawaiian Mission Children's Society and its Librarian, Elizabeth Larson, and to the Hawaiian Historical Society and its librarian, Barbara Dunn, for their help and cooperation regarding portions of the material and photography in this book, as well as granting me permission to reproduce same.

Further thanks go to the photo librarians at the Hawai'i Archives.

I am indebted to Mr. Robert Van Dyke for permission to reproduce his photo of the scrimshaw from his collection of Hawaiiana.

Additional information regarding the whaling era and what it meant to Hawai'i may be obtained by consulting the suggested reading list at the back of the book.

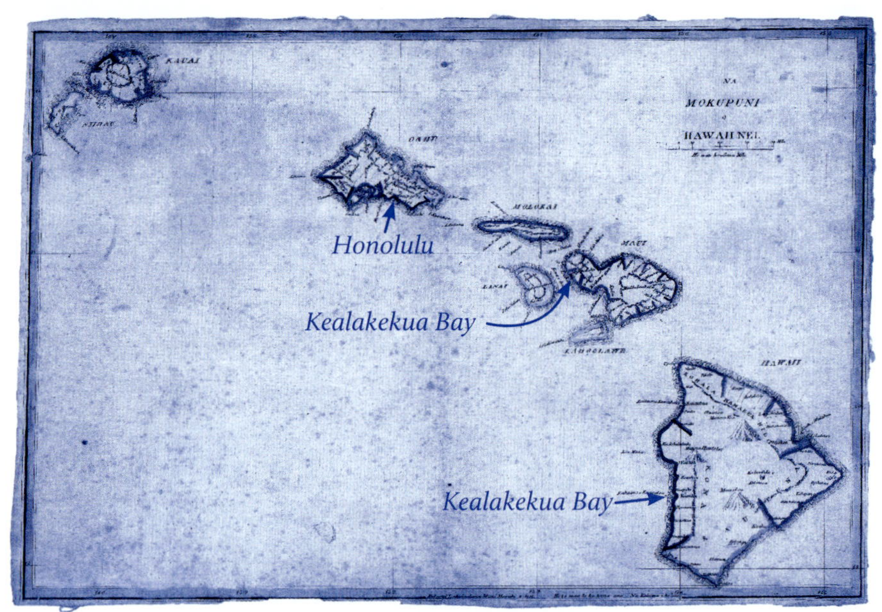

IN THE BEGINNING

there was a whale and two ships...

In October 1819 two New England ships, *Balaena* and *Equator,* cruising off the coast of Hawai'i's Kealakekua Bay, harpooned and killed a whale. They were the first American whalers to do so in Hawaiian waters, but they were certainly not to be the last. And it was only the beginning...

As new whaling territories were uncovered in Pacific and Arctic seas, numerous ships from New England ports came to dock at the harbors of Honolulu and Lahaina. They brought to Hawai'i not only riches but a philosophy as well. It was an arrogant philosophy, one well-known to seafaring men throughout the ports of the world. To those who would question its lawless practices, it declared that "there was no God west of Cape Horn."

During that same October, and half a world away, another ship carried a cargo that would change all that.

The ship was the brig *Thaddeus* from New England. Her cargo consisted of missionaries who had every intention of bringing

Above: Map of the Hawaiian Islands, 1837 by Simon P. Kalama. WIKIMEDIA
Opposite page: JEAN BUNGARTZ / WIKIMEDIA

God west of Cape Horn. They aimed not to catch whales but to save souls.

Leaving her stormy coastline behind, the *Thaddeus* headed toward the bluer waters of the Pacific and beyond to "Owyhee." The journey was a hard one. Ocean transportation in those days meant that such a trip could take anywhere from five to twelve months. Conditions aboard ship were less than desirable. Quarters were narrow, diet was unwholesome, seasickness an ever-present companion for most aboard. But there was no turning back for either whaler or missionary. Their destinies were converging and the proving ground would be Hawai'i.

That October 1819, an era began for Hawai'i in which whaler lawlessness and missionary law would clash again and again, racking the land with violence and causing Hawai'i's king many a weary and many a worried hour. No storyteller could have invented a drama with more conflict than the one played in Hawai'i during her wild, whaling days.

Riots, burnings, shootings...sailors armed with pistol, club and knife, threatening missionaries and native Hawaiians alike. Ships firing cannon on missionary homes. Police trying in vain to quell riots. Seamen demanding Island girls like so much merchandise—and willing to pay the price. Gambling, drunkenness, theft, venereal disease...

It was all a part of the colorful whaling history of Hawai'i.

PRE-WHALING, PRE-MISSIONARY HAWAI'I

Up to 1819, there had been only an occasional whaler from Great Britain and no missionaries, but all the same, foreigners were not new to the Hawaiians. Traders and merchant vessels had been visiting the Islands since the time of Captain Cook. King Kamehameha I, Hawai'i's first great monarch, had encouraged trade, especially in fur and sandalwood. The king, himself, held trade monopolies receiving all the income derived from the pork and sandalwood revenues. As trade increased, he appointed agents to act for him, finalizing trade agreements and collecting harbor fees from ships that docked.

A LAND WITHOUT RELIGION. The great King Kamehameha I died in May 1819, and as was then the custom, his bones were removed by a trusted chief and concealed in a cave. The throne passed to his son, young Liholiho, who became Kamehameha II. But the young king was not fated to rule alone as had his mighty father before him. The beautiful and domineering figure of his father's favorite wife, Ka'ahumanu, came between Liholiho and his people. Confronting him in warrior garb, she told him that it had been his father's desire that they rule the kingdom

Liholiho (left) and Ka'ahumanu (right). HAWAI'I STATE ARCHIVES

jointly. He, the king, would be the supreme power. Ka'ahumanu, as his Kuhina-nui or second in command, would assist him.

Ka'ahumanu's goal was power. But first she had to overthrow the law of the land or the "kapu" system, as it was called. The kapu system was a series of religious do's and don'ts, relating to sacred days, ceremonies, and rules and relationships among men, women, and the gods of Hawai'i. The laws relating to women were many and humiliating. Ka'ahumanu set out to conquer them.

THE OVERTHROW OF KAPU. Women were considered inferior to men—so much so that they were not even worthy to be sacrificed to the gods. Especially debasing were the kapu relating to women and food and eating. Certain foods were denied them, foods that were usually the tastiest and most delicate. And men and women were not allowed to eat together but had to have separate houses, stoves, and tables.

Slowly, Ka'ahumanu and the king's mother, Keōpūolani, worked on the young king to rid the land of the irksome kapu. The king held out but finally at a banquet one day, he went to the women's table. Before the shocked eyes of his subjects, he began to pile food into his mouth while sitting with the women. The high priest supported him. With lighted torch in hand, Hewahewa, the priest, set fire to the idols and heiaus of the land. The people followed the example. One by one, the kapu and the stone idols supporting them were destroyed. The old religion had gone.

It remained for the missionaries to give the people a new one.

Keōpūolani (center).
THE AMERICAN TRACT SOCIETY

HAWAI'I AND THE MISSIONARIES. Who were they and what did they want of the native Hawaiians—these well-meaning zealots of Christian theology? Intolerant, dogmatic, they were as uncompromising as their New England rocks. But they were also self-sacrificing and dedicated visionaries.

Word of the dark plight of the "native" had reached them through a young Hawaiian who in 1810 had been converted to Christianity while in New England. His name was Heneri Opukahaia, or "Henry Obookiah," as he was known to the New Englanders. "Obookiah" preached, wrote, and pleaded with the mission in New England to send missionaries to Hawai'i so that his people could be enlightened and turned from their idols and sacrifices toward the light of the Christian God. His many writings and lectures prompted the mission to send the first missionaries on the *Thaddeus* in October of 1819. By the time the *Thaddeus* reached Hawai'i, the missionaries found a land ripe for new religion and law. The old idols had been destroyed by the king, queen, and high priest. What remained was a Hawai'i without either law or religion. The men and women of the mission set to work at once.

Henry Obookiah. WIKIMEDIA

NEW WAYS, NEW THINGS. The *Thaddeus* had carried Reverends Bingham and Thurston, two ordained ministers and their wives; a physician, Dr. Holman and his wife; teachers Whitney and Ruggles and their wives; printer Loomis and his wife; farmer Chamberlain, his wife and five children; and four Hawaiian youths who had been converted to Christianity.

At first the missionary ways were ridiculed by Hawaiian ali'i and commoner alike. However, in a very short while, the missionaries had gained the Hawaiians' respect. Naturally, the wonder of new things helped. Windows, furniture, and clothes—not to mention minor miracles like books and writing—caused some native Hawaiians to look up to the missionary.

A New England missionary preaches in a kukui grove in Hawai'i, as depicted in an engraving appearing in Wilkes' Narrative of the United States Exploring Expedition. DRAWN BY ALFRED T. AGATE. ENGRAVED BY ROLPH, J. A. / WIKIMEDIA

The missionary's duties were many and varied. To teach meant bible study, sewing classes, reading, writing, stories, and song. Reading and writing had to be taught to the Hawaiians but there was no written language to work with. So, first began the learning of the Hawaiian language by the missionary, then the creation of an alphabet and written words in Hawaiian. Books and pamphlets containing religious literature and songs were printed and circulated, allowing the missionaries to educate the Hawaiians quickly and thoroughly. In a surprisingly short while, literacy was exceptionally high among the hitherto untutored Hawaiian. This was mainly due to both chiefly and missionary efforts in that direction.

However, in addition to passing on the practical and spiritual aspects of Protestant Christianity, the men and women of the mission had their own practical and domestic chores to accomplish. This meant building their own homes and making their own tools and furniture; for the missionary women, it meant sewing, gardening, cooking, and teaching the same skills, as they knew them, to the women of Hawai'i.

In her book, *Life and Times of Mrs. L.G. Thurston,* Mrs. Lucy Thurston, a missionary wife, describes the visit of King Liholiho to the mission house. It was then a humble cluster of thatched cottages containing planked seats and a window which caught the sun. Windows were new to the Hawaiians. Their huts were dark and had only the smallest openings—usually low doors—which required a person entering to stoop, indeed almost crawl, into the dark interior of the hut. A window which let the sun into a home was truly a great discovery. So were the rocking chairs, sofas, and curtains made by the mission men and women.

The king wandered through the mission house impressed by the furnishings. *The piece de resistance* was a feather bed which caught Liholiho's fancy. The softness of it was a new thing to him. Another item that enticed him was the handcart the missionaries used. He promptly seated himself and had his men take him for a ride back to the village.

Drawing of Mrs. Lucy G. Thurston (1795–1876) on the lanai of her house reading the Bible.
WIKIMEDIA

Although in the beginning the missionaries had their share of enemies among the chiefs, they were quickly accepted when the Hawaiians noted their industry coupled by the fact that they had brought wives and children to settle down and work in the new land.

Obookiah, the man who had started things moving, had died in 1818 at the age of twenty-six. Two years later, a Kailua and a Honolulu mission started and in 1823, a Lahaina, Maui, mission was begun. To the missionaries, Obookiah had spoken truly: there was plenty of God's work for them in the Islands.

"Lancing a sperm whale." The crew of a whaleboat attempts a capture. It was not unusual for a thrashing whale to upset a small boat, throwing the men into the water. WIKIMEDIA

HAWAI'I AND THE WHALERS

It was another story with the whalers.

After the *Balaena* and *Equator,* it was only a matter of time before Hawai'i would be visited by vast numbers of whaling and merchant vessels. The day would come when the harbors at Honolulu and Lahaina would be crowded with ships, each rubbing decks with its neighbor. Indeed, anyone with a mind to do it could hop from one end of the harbor to another by using the decks of the different ships.

NEW TERRITORIES. The Atlantic whale had been hunted to scarcity and it was now the turn of the Pacific whale. That autumn, a new sperm whaling ground had been discovered off Japan's coast. Whaling ships began to dot the waters of the Pacific in search of the precious sperm oil and whale bone. A ship's voyage was lengthy—sometimes as long as three or four years. In that time, ships needed a place to dock for repairs, re-provisioning, and relaxation. Since Japan's ports were closed to foreigners, the ports of Honolulu and Lahaina quickly became the whaling centers of the Pacific.

Honolulu began by having approximately sixty whalers in 1822. As new whaling territories were found in Northern Pacific waters, the number of ships visiting the Islands gradually rose to over 140 annually. However, all arrivals did not mean all different ships. Often the same ships docked at the harbors several times during the season. But the figures represented quite a spurt of growth. In contrast to the sixty whalers in 1822, by 1846, the Islands had 596 ship arrivals: 167 at Honolulu and 429 at Lahaina.

NEW LIFESTYLES. As in the case of the gold rush towns of America, riches lay not only in gathering "gold"—which in this case was whale oil and whale bone—but also in supplying needs. Firewood was badly needed for ships and it was brought to town from the forests of O'ahu and Maui. The demand was so great that before long the forests were stripped and depleted. Typical of a "boomtown" atmosphere was the ecological abuse that occurred. Hawai'i was no different from the gold rush towns in that instance. Ecological considerations took a back seat to economics.

The ships came in spring and fall and were supplied with pork, fowls, vegetables, salt, rope, wood, and fresh water. New foods and new products sprang up to supply new needs: whalers could not or would not subsist on a diet of coconuts, fish, and poi. Because of the great demand of the ships for beef, Mexican cowboys were brought to Hawai'i in 1830 to teach the art of cattle ranching to

Cattle ranching, Parker Ranch, Hawai'i Island. HAWAI'I STATE ARCHIVES

David Kuloloia, 1930s. HAWAI'I STATE ARCHIVES

the Islands' cowhands. The Hawaiians called them "paniolas," after the Spanish, español. And, in 1840, the Irish potato was introduced to Hawaiian soil and flourished on the Kula lowlands of Maui.

All of the supplies came from the country people and were brought on the dusty, muddy, unpaved roads into the booming harbors of Honolulu and Lahaina. And once again, ecological and aesthetic niceties were pushed aside in favor of demand. In spite of the residents' disgust, cattle were driven through the main streets of the town and then to the port where they were slaughtered as they were needed.

The average Hawaiian still stuck pretty much to an Island diet of taro, sweet potatoes, and fish. Fruits like bananas, yams, and breadfruit and animals like pigs and chickens were produced for export and traded with ships. The natives made do with shellfish, crabs, and seaweed. Fishponds were then abundant in Hawai'i and fish was the staple. Chicken, pig, or dog might be eaten at a lū'au, prepared Island-style, surrounded by taro leaves and fragrant sweet potatoes and baked in one big pot or calabash.

Moli'i Fishponds, O'ahu. HAWAI'I STATE ARCHIVES

Whaling brought much money to the Islands and much new industry. Whaling vessels carrying huge amounts of oil and bone trans-shipped their valuable cargos to New England-bound vessels. This made it possible for them to empty their holds and get right back to the business of hunting whale while their precious cargo was en route to lucrative markets. And it increased the importance of Honolulu. Since it was the only port with ship repairing facilities, Honolulu catered to many merchant vessels as well as whalers.

The sailors spent money. Mark Twain in his *Letters from the Sandwich Islands* gave the figure spent by seamen in Honolulu in 1865 as $150,000 (an extremely high sum in those days). New industries catering to shipowners, ships' agents, captains, crews, and merchants were started. Sailmakers flourished as did blacksmiths and carpenters. The needs of the seafaring population created laundries, bakeries, retail outlets, small boarding houses, and mercantile establishments.

And whaling brought the outside world into the ports of Honolulu and Lahaina via the ships. For now, not only foreigners bought foreign made items, but local people wanted them, too. Inevitably, fashions changed, and the old ways were fast disappearing.

But Hawaiʻi was paying a high price for prosperity. The wealth that whaling brought was dependent solely on the ships and foreign commerce, and not on local agriculture and native Hawaiian skills. And these were suffering. Many young men were leaving the Islands. They came from the farms and villages and got jobs aboard the ships. Some of them shipped out as crew on foreign vessels. Many never returned to the Islands. To an agricultural community, such a state of affairs was highly undesirable.

But perhaps worse was the lowered moral and social quality of life which whaling fostered. An overflow—an invasion really—of hardened seamen flooded the port towns of Honolulu and Lahaina. The weather-beaten men were determined on whiskey and women, taking their pleasure where and in any way it could be found. Grogshops, brothels, and the philosophy of "no God west of the Horn" set the tone of life in the ports, making the atmosphere unacceptable to not only the missionary but to conservative islanders and foreign residents.

THE SAILORS LOT

The work of a seaman aboard a whaling vessel was grueling. Any slacking on the job resulted in a docking of allowance or in unpleasant duties such as stints at the wheel or duty aloft the mast. Labor was a never-ending process. Repairing rigging, ropes, and sails, spinning yarn for the many uses aboard ship, and generally keeping the vessel in trim shape could account for many of the sailor's hours at sea.

Both captain and crew were paid according to a share in the profits of the catch. Such a share was known as a "lay." Seamen would get a long lay as a share in the profits of the whale oil and whale bone catch. A long lay might comprise the 120th part of the entire catch. In proportion to rank, the captain and his officers would get shorter lays. A captain's lay, or share of the catch, could run anywhere from one-tenth to one-fourteenth. The finances of whaling did not usually favor the seamen and many times not even the captain. It was the shipowner who usually came out ahead, since all sorts of provisions and stipulations were attached to the lays of both captain and crew. But though the system had its evils, the profit-sharing idea did increase the individual crewman's initiative and sense of responsibility for the ship.

Above: Sailors on board.

Sailor's language, understandably enough, was salty even when referring to non-nautical items. Ditties, phrases, and catchwords were used in great part. Though not always respectable, the sailor's lingo never lacked for descriptive quality.

A seaman's diet had not much to recommend it. Salt pork, mush, hard bread, and meat were the mainstays. There was no milk. Some fruit and vegetables were offered to guard against scurvy, but these were scarcely given in plentiful supply. Indispensable to the sailor was his tobacco. It was more than just a smoke; it was his companion, tiding him through a lonely night watch under the stars.

Sailor wearing a monkey jacket, mid to late ninteenth century. THE NAVY & MARINE LIVING HISTORY ASSOCIATION / WIKIMEDIA

Aboard every whaling ship were two other indispensables. One was a medicine chest and the other a slop chest. The medicine chest was what the name implied; the slop chest was exactly the opposite. Contrary to its name, it was a necessity for the well-groomed sailor, since it stocked all sorts of sundries and dry goods which the seamen would need for the long voyage. Stock included hats, shoes, handkerchiefs, pea jackets, monkey jackets, trousers, shawls, belts, shirts, toilet articles, soaps, sewing thread, stationery, tobacco, etc. Supposedly, slop chest goods were to be sold at only a slightly higher price than their original cost, so that the seamen could benefit economically. Actually, it was the other way around. The men were fleeced. Goods were sold at the most inflated prices, especially after the ship had been out on the waters for a period of a year or more. It was then that the prices shot up. And, after all, the men were captive buyers. It was slop chest or nothing for the much needed knife or pair of shoes or pants. The outrageous price of slop chest articles was a major grievance on most of the whaling vessels.

Perhaps because of such high prices the sailors became expert tailors. Sailors' clothes were colorful if nothing else. The men often darned with different colored patches so that a single outfit might boast an infinite variety of color and pattern. The men wore very wide pants which were held tight to the waist and secured by a belt which buckled. The belt had a dual purpose—it not only held up the sailor's pants but provided a place for him to hold his knife as well. And his knife was essential. Used by the sailor as an all around tool, it also served as his dinner utensil.

The social hour at sea was supper. Times were from 6:00 to 8:00 p.m. It was then that the sailor could relax. After eating, the men came out on deck to enjoy the evening. Entertaining each other, they sang nautical ditties and told tall stories. Invariably, there was a fiddler or musician in the crew. While he played, the men danced with each other or sang songs.

There were libraries aboard ship, places where a sailor could read a book or two—if he knew how to read. Or rooms where he could get stationery and writing materials. Many a whaling ship had a carpentry shop as well. Such a "shop" might consist of nothing more than a workbench, some tools, a turning lathe, and smaller items. If there was no carpentry shop, or if a seaman cared not to read and write, he could indulge his creative talents by taking up his knife and scrimshawing. Scrimshaw, the art of carving on a hard surface, lent itself to artistic renderings on the teeth or jawbone of the whale. Scrimshawed whales' teeth made highly attractive and merchandisable gift items—especially after they had been polished to a high gloss.

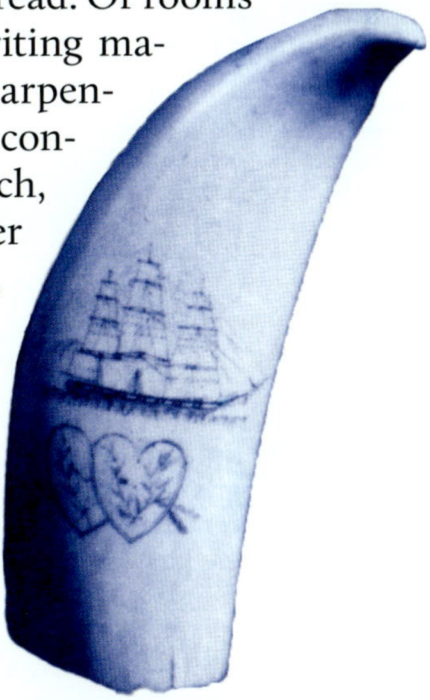

Scrimshaw, the art of carving on a hard surface, was especially suited to artistic renderings on whales' teeth. ROBERT VAN DYKE

Such recreations, however, were but a small break in the monotonous and backbreaking schedule of a seaman. Not only was the work exhausting, but the sailor who had the bad luck to take sick was at the mercy of the medical and surgical expertise of the doctor-captain of the ship. Many times, the diagnosis was somewhat less than skillful. Still, the captain was nothing if not a methodical "doctor." His medicine bottles were numbered and each number could be checked against a master list which gave the properties of the medicine and what it would be best used for. If the seaman survived his "doctor," he convalesced in the tightest confinement possible. Quarters were narrow and stifling. In stormy weather, everything around him not only creaked but might fly at him in his sickbed.

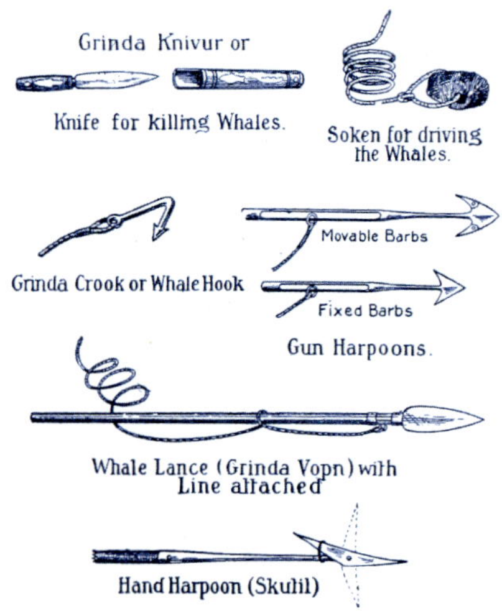

JEAFFRESON, JOSEPH RUSSELL, ORIGINAL HELD BY THE BRITISH LIBRARY / WIKIMEDIA

A common grievance and cause for desertion among the sailors was the captain's curtailing of supplies and food. A ship might be at sea for nearly a year and in all that time never have even gotten close to a whale. Still, she would be due for provisions and repairs. To have to re-provision without a catch was a state of affairs no captain courted. A captain in danger of such a situation would begin to ration out smaller and smaller portions of everything to the crew. The men might be touching starvation's door, but they would receive no more than he had a mind to give—unless they stole it or by some miracle got a catch.

A typical trip for a whaler might go something like this: the ship would take off for the North Seas which was about a seven month voyage. Then, she would return to Honolulu. While in port, she would transship her oil to homeward-bound vessels. The rest of the time would be spent in refitting, repairing and re-provisioning. When she was shipshape once again, she would sail to California in search of humpback whales, returning once more to Honolulu to load up with fruits and vegetables so as to prevent scurvy from striking the crew. At this time, the men would probably be given shore leave. For a few days, they raised hell at the port of Honolulu or Lahaina and then they were off on the next trip—this time to the north via Japan in search of the sperm whale.

THE CATCH

A whaling vessel might have thirty-one men compared to a merchant ship's fifteen. She would carry four or five boats which were made of a light cedar and usually manned by about four crewmen who would take off as soon as the whale was sighted. The remainder of the crew waited aboard the mother ship.

The moment the cry signaling whales was heard, boats were lowered. The chase began. With much yelling (most of it colorful if not downright profane) the boat steerer urged the crew onward. At first the men were cautious. Premature action might scare off the whale. However, as they got closer and closer to the whale, they increased speed, manning oars with high energy to the spot where the boat steerer could throw the harpoon.

A successful throw meant that the harpoon had successfully pierced the whale's body. Boat and whale were now fated to fight it out and the chase began. The whale might dive. Or it might choose to use its flukes (tail). Either action could spell the death of the boat. A deft maneuver by a whale with those massive flukes could easily smash a light whaleboat, leaving nothing but splinters floating on the water. Sometimes, the crew would be forced to

DRAWN BY FRANCIS ALLYN OLMSTED. LITHOGRAPH OF ENDICOTT, N.Y. / WIKIMEDIA

abandon the boat, sacrificing the catch, so as to save themselves. For, a whale could lift an entire boat on its back! In such instances when a boat was demolished, the crew was thrown into the sea, only to thrash through turbulent waters while still encumbered by pea jackets and heavy whaling boots.

Another danger was the rope attached to the harpoon. A man's arm or leg might tangle in the lightning coil when the action got hot. If that happened, the sailor could be jerked by an arm or leg and thrown over the side.

Even after a whale was successfully harpooned, it could still be very active. It might easily swim for many miles, dragging the whaleboat along with it at great speed. This romp through the briny by whale and boat was known among seamen as the "Nantucket Sleighride." However, sooner or later, the sleighride would have to end and then the steersman would complete the kill, using his lance.

Often, the wounded whale flung himself wildly about in the sea, bloodying the water around him in a last effort to save himself. As if paying homage to such fighting spirit, the boat drew away and waited in the distance until the struggle was over.

The captured whale was then "waifed," which simply meant that a small identifying rod with a conspicuous flag was stuck into him so that he could later be found again. Even so large an animal might be camouflaged by the sea around him. Meanwhile, he floated on the water, suitably tagged and identified while his killers searched for others like him in the area.

So much for the successful harpooning and kill. Not all were successful. If fortune did not favor the captain and crew, an unsuccessful effort might go something like this: Instead of grabbing or skinning into the whale's back, the boat steerer's harpoon might slide harmlessly across the whale's body and the whale might dive. A bad loss. Approximately seventy barrels of oil—if it is a sperm whale, or in dollars $2,300.00. Needless to say, the boat steerer would be wise to walk carefully and look behind him. He is hardly the most popular member of the crew after a miss. Another such instance, and he will lose his job and be turned before the mast while someone else takes over his duties.

Sometimes, even after harpooning was accomplished and a kill was made, the whale could become waterlogged and the heavy carcass might sink to the bottom of the sea where it would profit no one but the sharks. For not only was valuable oil and bone lost, but indispensable weapons such as harpoons, lances, and rope.

Sharks were a very real scare. A whale might be already secured alongside the ship, the crewman might be inserting the blubber hook into him, and look up from his task to see sharks moving in quickly, attracted by the scent of blood. Once the sharks smelled blood, both whale and man were in danger of being the next meal of this relentless predator.

Indeed, there was no lack of danger at any of the stages of capturing a whale. From the sighting to harpooning to the kill, and finally, to the securing of the whale and removal of oil and blubber, serving as a member of a whaling crew was not a job for those thin in courage or physical endurance.

Searching for whales from a ship's crow's nest. FROM *HUNTING AND TRAPPING STORIES; A BOOK FOR BOYS*

THE CUTTING IN

In her journal, *The Captain's Best Mate,* Mary Chipman Lawrence, wife of a whaling captain, said that one could read a description of a whale but still have no concept of the marvel unless it was personally seen. But even without a personal experience, the riches of the monster are brought home when one learns that the head of a right whale contains 1,500 pounds of bone and the tongue no less than ten barrels of oil.

After the kill, the whale was towed back to the ship and the operation known as the "cutting-in" was started.

Sperm oil, which came from the "case" or cavity of the whale, was located in the upper part of the head. When it was not expedient for the whale's head to be raised on deck, the oil was often bailed out of the head while the whale was still tied alongside the ship. The head cavity of a large sperm whale—one about eighty feet long—contained at least ten barrels of oil. Blubber was removed from the body with the aid of ropes, iron hooks, spades, and other tools of the trade. It was cut into small pieces and taken to the tryworks. These were brick furnaces containing two huge iron cauldrons in which the blubber was

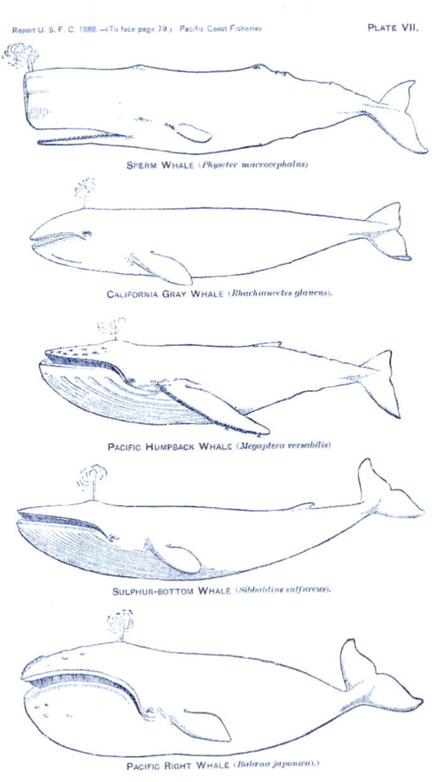

Sperm Whale (Physeter macrocephalus); *California Gray Whale* (Rhachianectes glaucus); *Pacific Humpback Whale* (Megaptera versabilis); *Sulphur-Bottom Whale* (Sibbaldius sulfureus); *Pacific Right Whale* (Balaenia japonica).
FRESHWATER AND MARINE IMAGE BANK AT THE UNIVERSITY OF WASHINGTON. / WIKIMEDIA

Cutting in. The whale is tied alongside the ship, and the blubber is removed.

Converting blubber into oil by chopping and boiling smaller pieces in the Trypots. WILLIAM M. DAVIS / WIKIMEDIA

boiled so as to remove impurities. Then it was cooled, strained, and finally stored into casks aboard ship.

Whale's teeth were valuable as well as the oil and bone. Teeth, when carved or scrimshawed into artworks and jewelry, found a good buyers' market. But before they could be marketed, they had to be taken from the whale.

Pulling whale's teeth had its intricacies. While the whale's lower jaw was bound to ring bolts in the deck, several men performed the "surgery" using both hands. The boat steerer (that same fellow who used the harpoon) wielded a tool called a cutting spade and applied it to the teeth. The rest of the equipment consisted of two pulleys manned by the sailors. Thus, the dental experts stood ready. At a signal from the head man—the signal was typically nautical, a short ditty or pungent three word phrase—the operation commenced. Spade was applied, the pulleys pulled, and the teeth snapped out like peas from a pod. Being already dead, the patient felt no pain. Such was the highly automated and painless dentistry of pulling whales' teeth.

NO GOD WEST OF THE HORN

no more fiddling or dancing on the Sabbath...
no more going for horse rides on the Sabbath...
no more shooting pool for money...
no more gambling...
no more licensing of grogshops...
no more rum...
no more taking girls out to the ships...
no more...

In 1825, whalemen visiting Honolulu were in an ugly state of mind. What before had been an Island kingdom with easygoing morals was now a stronghold of puritanism. With the aid of the missionaries, Queen Kaʻahumanu and her able minister, Chief Kalanimoku, had put forth a new code of laws based upon the Ten Commandments. The laws prohibited drinking, gambling, and prostitution, as well as such lesser vices as fiddling and dancing and riding a horse on the Sabbath. Most aggravating were the laws governing women. Once available Island girls were forbidden to go out to ships with the men.

Chief Kalanimoku, 1768-1827.
LOUIS CHORIS, HAWAIʻI STATE ARCHIVES

Kamehameha III (Kauikeaouli), a wild young man, he finally settled down to rule a kingdom. Kamehameha III reigned for over thirty years—the longest of any Hawaiian monarch.
HAWAIʻI STATE ARCHIVES

Hawaiʻi was now ruled by a regency. Kamehameha II and his Queen had died of the measles while touring England in 1824. Young King Kauikeaouli, a boy of twelve, became Kamehameha III. However, he was still a minor and the country was ruled by Kaʻahumanu and her Minister who allied themselves with the missionaries and the new laws.

This was not the case with some other chiefs. Boki, governor of O'ahu, and his beautiful wife, Liliha, were an example. Had it been possible, they would have overthrown Ka'ahumanu and her Minister. Not only did they not support the missionary way of life, but they themselves owned a grogshop or two.

Law being what it is, there were ways to get around it. The members of the foreign community were experts at circumventing unpopular laws. One way was to obtain grog for a sailor at a black market cost. For those who craved the "spirits," the salesman always knew where some rum could be gotten. He was more than willing to let the customer in on the secret—for a price. The price was excessive, well over what the item was actually worth on the market. But if the customer could not come to the grogshop, why then the grogshop would come to the customer.

On the Island of Maui, there were worse problems than "spirits."

In Lahaina town, the captain of the *Daniel,* an English whaling vessel, had paid in gold for a young Hawaiian girl and had taken her aboard his ship and had sailed away. Incensed and shocked by such action, missionaries Richards and Chamberlain prevailed on the Island chiefs to right the situation. The chiefs agreed that it was wrong for Hawaiians to make money off their daughters. Promptly, they passed the law forbidding the girls to go out to the ships.

When the *Daniel* returned to Lahaina, the men were furious when they heard of the new law. Storming en masse to the house of missionary Richards, they demanded a repeal of the law. Demand was perhaps too mild a word—threat would be closer to the mark. Richards refused to be intimidated. He diplomatically referred them to the governor and chiefs of Maui. These were the lawmakers. Any grievances the sailors had must be taken up with the proper authorities.

The sailors answered Richards. They threatened to burn down his house and to murder him, his wife, and his child. Frail, delicate Mrs. Richards stood beside her husband. Together they faced the angry men. If necessary, they would die together. At this show of courage the sailors left without harming them.

Two days later, they were back. This time, they came in a raiding party armed with pistols and knives. But they hadn't reckoned on the Hawaiians. It was then, said Mrs. Lucy Thurston in her book, that the people known to the missionaries as "barbarians" and "savages" defended their teachers with their lives. Hoapili, a chief of the first class on Maui, had his men form a tight guard around the Richards. Day and night, they protected the missionaries by standing guard, bayonets pointed out. Chief Hoapili infused his men with moral support by stating that if anyone shot his teachers, the ball would have to pass first through his own body.

The devotion of the Hawaiians did not go unnoticed—either by the missionaries or the captain and crew of the *Daniel.* Richards and his family were unharmed. Eventually, the sailors sailed away from Lahaina, without having had any of the Island women.

Another incident occurred in 1826 when the ship, *Dolphin,* skippered by Captain John Percival, sailed into Honolulu on a mission to clear up some sandalwood debts and to search for a band of mutineers.

Naturally, the crew wanted women. But the law was being enforced. Five women who had flouted authority were being punished. Each of the women had to carry ten stones for the Church.

Missionary William Richards and his wife Clarissa Lyman Richards. Aided by courageous Hawaiians, they defied the threats of an angry mob of whalers. WIKIMEDIA

The captain of the *Dolphin* talked with the regent, Ka'ahumanu, begging her to stretch the laws regarding sailors and women, but she would not. Ka'ahumanu continued to maintain that a stranger must obey the laws of the country he was in and that these laws would save her people from ruin.

No respecters of the law, the sailors rioted. They broke into the homes of ailing minister Kalanimoku and missionary Hiram Bingham. Fortunately, Captain Percival had arrived at the scene of the riot in time to prevent tragedy. Reverend Bingham had been assaulted but not really hurt, and no one else had been killed or seriously wounded. To be on the safe side, the captain had the men promptly imprisoned. The whole incident gave Governor Boki food for thought. He was shaken by the riot, and he relaxed the law prohibiting traffic between the sailors and girls.

Rev. Hiram Bingham and Mrs. Sybil (Moseley) Bingham. HAWAIʻI STATE ARCHIVES

But by no means was this the last incident.

In 1827, the ship, *John Palmer,* visited at Lahaina. Despite the law, some Island girls went out to the ship. Governor Hoapili of Maui requested of the captain that the women be sent back. The captain ignored his request. For three days, Hoapili was patient. At the end of that time and after repeated refusals, he lost his patience and had the captain's shore boat seized.

Alarmed, the captain made straight for missionary Richard's house. He gave Richards an ultimatum. If Hoapili refused to let him return to his ship, the crew would fire on the town of Lahaina. A meeting of all concerned was held at the governor's house. It ended with an agreement that the next morning the captain would have his boat back.

Things did not happen in quite that way, however. The moment that the captain regained his boat and headed back to his ship, the *John Palmer* began to fire on Lahaina town anyway. She trained her cannon specifically on the house of missionary Richards, firing several times. Richards took shelter in his cellar and escaped being hurt. Finally, when the captain came near enough to the ship, he ordered it to cease its firing.

But the conduct of the whalers was not the only trouble the kingdom faced. To add to the problems of the land, the strong regent Kaʻahumanu died in 1832. Kauikeaouli, the young king, was now Kamehameha Ill, ruler of the kingdom of Hawai'i. His Kuhina-nui or second in command was Chiefess Kīna'u, one of the wives of Kamehameha II. She proceeded to follow Ka'ahumanu's example in espousing missionary ways.

John (Ioane) Kaneiakama Papa 'Ī'ī (1800–1870). WIKIMEDIA

Kauikeaouli and Kīna'u quarreled frequently. The young king took the side of pleasure-loving Liliha and a young, debauched Tahitian named Kaomi. A wild era returned to the Island. Distilleries were started once again while schools and churches were abandoned and neglected. The kingdom was split by the two factions. The king and his companions wanted their pleasures while Kīna'u and Hoapili worked for law and order. Indeed, Hoapili became a one-man vice squad. He made it his mission to personally destroy the distilleries on O'ahu.

Eventually, the king matured, turning from the licentious influences of Liliha and Kaomi. He decided to work in harmony with Kīna'u. Differences between them were resolved. Aided by the missionaries and governors of each Island, the two now conducted affairs of state in unity.

Timoteo or Timothy Kamalehua Ha'alilio (1808–1844). HAWAI'I STATE ARCHIVES

The king was aided by not only missionaries but by young and educated Hawaiians as well. David Malo, John Papa 'Ī'ī, and Timothy Ha'alilio were scholars and patriots. Neither puritans nor pleasure seekers, they were knowledgeable men who wished to preserve the monarchy while realizing the need for a law code with teeth. This was finally accomplished. By 1839, Hawai'i had a civil code and a Declaration of Rights; by 1840 it had its first Constitution.

The Hawaiian kingdom had come a long way from the autocratic days of the just but dictatorial Kamehameha I. But it still had a long way to go.

HONOLULU, HOW IT LOOKED TO VISITORS

1834. Young doctor Frederick Bennett, on a whaling trip around the world, was captivated by Honolulu's lush garden valleys and its fertile yields of grapes, potatoes, yams, bananas, figs, and other fruits and vegetables.

Honolulu town had outdoor markets by the seaside where Islanders sold their produce. Due to the influx of foreigners exercising various trades, there were many well-stocked shops with a variety of supplies to suit any seaman's needs. There were also hotels, boarding houses, auction houses, poolrooms, theatres, bowling alleys, grogshops, gambling dens, and brothels.

1840. Francis Allyn Olmsted a young surgeon traveling on a whaler, had a keen eye for detail. In his journal, he devoted much space to Honolulu fashions.

Island dress was interesting—to say the least. Kapa, the native cloth, though rarely seen any more by itself, made an occasional appearance in combination with a European garment. A man might wear a kapa malo (a light Island wrap around the waist) but

Above: Queen Kīnaʻu and her retinue of muʻumuʻu-clad ladies return from services at Kawaiahaʻo Church. HAWAIʻI STATE ARCHIVES

above that article he would be wearing a heavy sailor's pea jacket. Though the sun might scorch the street and its inhabitants, the pea jacket would stay on. Another man might wear a kapa mantle, a garb which strongly suggested bare feet or at the very least a pair of light sandals. Instead, the man would have on a pair of heavy whaling boots.

The women, less concerned with status, wore the mu'umu'u, a gown which looked like a long and loose nightdress and which had been introduced to them by the missionaries. Dresses were made of European silks and satins. Black silk was an Island favorite. A bright shawl might be tacked at the waist while feathers, flowers, or a high tortoise-shell comb were worn in the hair. And Island hair which had previously hung loose and relaxed in the wind now was elaborately curled and coiffed.

High ranking chiefs' wives wore feather headdresses. These were made of beautiful, brightly-colored feathers arranged in a thick roll in their natural colors from the birds. Indeed, bird feathers were so valuable as to be used for currency. Often, they were fastened together in small bunches to be paid to chiefs as currency for taxes.

Younger women with less exalted rank had to be content with flowered headdresses. Both men and women wore flowered lei around their necks.

The chiefs and those in positions of authority wore blue broadcloth uniforms patterned after British naval and military people.

1857. Mary Chipman Lawrence had probably seen more of the world than many of the women of her acquaintance. She and her small daughter had spent much time aboard her husband's whaling vessel. She was familiar with the colorful language and she had seen for herself how whales were caught, killed, and cut up. But although she had seen a less "genteel" side of life, she was not prepared for certain features of Hawaiian existence.

Very much a product of a cloistered New England environment, the lady was disturbed by the idea that the natives lived together with no apartments or separate quarters in their homes. Nor could she adjust to the fact that many of them wore no clothing in their homes or that the men and women bathed together.

1866. A young reporter named Samuel Clemens who also answered to the name of Mark Twain paid thirteen dollars for a horse in Hawai'i and took a ride through Honolulu town one Saturday afternoon in April 1866.

The sights and sounds of the marketplace captivated him. Saturday was the day Island folk dressed and came into town. Men and girls in their finery crowded the streets. The girls wore fine black silks or robes of flowing reds or whites. Their hair was caught up in nets and their hats decorated with fresh flowers. Around their necks were lei of red 'ōhia flowers fashioned by their own hands; they had dusky throats and smelled like thunder with "their villainous cocoa-nut oil."

The young journalist set it all down and promptly mailed it to his Sacramento newspaper as part of his *Letters From The Sandwich Islands.* He was especially taken with the pā'ū riders, women on horseback, "their gaudy riding habits streaming like banners behind them...floating and flapping behind on both sides beyond the horse's tail like a couple of fancy flags...." He described the riding postures. The girls sat their horses like Major-Generals, throwing their chests out, and sweeping by him like the wind.

Mark Twain had this and a great deal more to say about the Hawai'i of that time—not all of it complimentary. But, perhaps Hawai'i had such an effect on visitors of that age. Few seemed capable of a neutral attitude. Opinions were fairly emotional and usually extremely subjective.

The first 'Iolani Palace. In 1878, it was torn down and replaced by the present palace. HAWAI'I STATE ARCHIVES

THE SAILORS' RIOT

In November 1852, the town of Honolulu hosted more than 200 ships and over 3,000 sailors. The whaling fleet had returned from the north and the men were celebrating. The town was a beehive of activity. So was the jail. Guards were kept busy disciplining drunk and disorderly sailors.

On the night of November 8, Henry Burns, a drunken sailor off the *Emerald,* was murdered in his cell by a prison guard. Burns had been fighting with his cellmate and tearing up the bricks from the floor of his cell. When George Sherman, the guard on duty, tried to quiet him, Burns would not be quieted. He threatened Sherman. Sherman retaliated by striking him on the head with a club. Burns fell unconscious to the floor of his cell. Next morning, he was dead.

The death of Henry Burns was all that was needed to trigger enmities. Throughout the overcrowded port, the news quickly spread

The hard, monotonous shipboard life fostered a breed of men who were restless and pleasure-starved. Once ashore, they threw law and order to the winds and sought out grogshop and brothel. Many spent their shore leaves in Honolulu's Fort or prison. THE BETTMANN ARCHIVE

like a lit match touched to oil. Seamen gathered in crowds at the grogshops and on the street corners to discuss it. The mood was hostile. The men blamed the police and the Hawaiian government.

George Sherman was locked up in the Fort for his own safety.

An inquest was held. A jury composed of five shipmasters and five residents of the town agreed that Henry Burns' death had been the result of a blow to the head.

No one doubted that Sherman had been the one to inflict the blow. Sherman's plea was that he had not acted out of malice but simply to defend himself from Burns. Such a method of self-defense was questionable—at least the jury must have thought so. The wording of the official verdict was that Sherman had used his club in "cowardice" to quell the disturbance. In the end, Sherman was held on a charge of manslaughter.

When news of the verdict got out, Honolulu was invaded by sailors. Boatload after boatload left their ships. Like a conquering army they gathered around the Fort, screaming for Sherman. The words of the authorities fell on deaf ears. Promises of justice by trial were treated with contempt. Nothing would calm them.

Residents of the town waited anxiously.

Burns' funeral was held on the afternoon of November 10 at Nu'uanu Cemetery. Several thousand sailors marched as mourners in a long procession to the cemetery. Immediately after the funeral, they made straight for the grogshops and drank themselves into a rage. From then on, Honolulu was a town controlled by drink-maddened men.

Hordes gathered at the street corners, shouting and screaming that they would raid the Fort and hang all the policemen. Some of the shipmasters thought to calm the men by trying to reason with them. They made speeches at the corner of Fort and Merchant Street. In vain. Neither they nor any other authority, including the American Consul, could get through to the now uncontrollable mob.

That evening, some of the mob decided to rescue a sailor whom the police were holding in a police station near the waterfront.

They raided the station, wrecking furniture and destroying anything in their path. Whatever looked valuable they took. The policemen fought bravely, but they were outnumbered and they knew it. Suddenly, where before there had been a mob, there was

now a minor army, a murderous brigade of men using axes, clubs, and other deadly weapons.

Finally, when the sailors had sufficiently ravaged the station, they set fire to it.

And in doing so almost burned down Honolulu Harbor.

For the fire had spread from the station to two adjoining buildings and the flames had begun moving toward a nearby ship. The ships sat like so many sardines in the overcrowded harbor. It needed only one to be set ablaze—and the rest would have shot up with it, affording the residents the sight of one mighty conflagration. Luckily, they were spared the spectacle. The wind shifted, diverting the path of the flames.

The police station and the adjoining buildings had burned to ashes. The hand-operated fire engine which had been used to fight the fire had done little more than keep the men busy that were using it. The station and the buildings were gone.

By now, the drunken mob had thrown law and order to the winds. Through the night, they roamed the streets in packs, going from one grogshop to another, drinking and shouting, "charge it!" when the bartender presented them their bill. Nor did they limit themselves to the grogshops, but forced their way into private homes, making themselves the "guests" of the families gathered within.

The residents were alarmed. Fearful of further antagonizing the already incensed men, several families made a show of courtesy. Some had "anticipated" and wisely had cakes and drinks prepared for their "guests." A Dr. Hoffman proceeded to serve beer to the sailors and then sat down and played piano for them. Drunk as they were, the men must have appreciated the good doctor's concertizing. When he had finished entertaining them, they politely thanked him and left his house quietly and courteously.

Where were the government and the police when all this was going on? Out of sight—on orders from the governor. The town's law enforcement facilities were no match for such a mob.

However, the residents and shipmasters had not been altogether idle. A series of meetings had been held at the Fort. Discussions had proceeded and the authorities decided that the town would not be put under martial law but instead a citizens guard should be formed. Such a guard would number about 200 men and these would be stationed in strategic parts of town during the nights. As a further discouragement to violence, an additional 300 armed natives and a police force were to be kept at the Fort.

Slowly, the riot wound down. Slowly, the streets were flushed of the small pockets of insurrectionists. One sailor, trying to pry open a reservoir with a crow bar, was apprehended by the police. Rioters were still present but were gradually and inevitably rounded up by the citizens guard. Men began to scatter instead of congregating. Sailors made their way furtively back to their ships. The more stubborn were forced out of their boarding house rooms by constables. Any sailor with no pass or authorized discharge was promptly arrested. Subsequently, the ringleaders of the riot were jailed. With them out of the picture, the 1852 riot was ended.

And what of George Sherman? The man who had struck the fatal blow; he who had been the indirect cause of the burning, looting, and narrowlymissed destruction of Honolulu Harbor? What finally happened to him? Sherman served time for manslaughter but was eventually released. Once more a free man, he took up the honest occupation of shoemaker and saddler and made his permanent home in Hawai'i.

THE FORGOTTEN MEN

Whaling and merchant men were the orphans of the world, the wanderers of the age; the forgotten men of each new port they visited. Who was there to care whether they lived or died? In a strange port they had no one but their shipmates and the dubious recreations found in grogshop and brothel. Adrift from family and friends, far from the stabilizing influence of home, for the sailor there was still "no God west of Cape Horn."

Then, something happened to change all that.

Correspondence had been exchanged for several years between the missionaries in Hawai'i and the American Seamen's Friend Society of New York. The subject had been the establishment of a sailors' chaplain in Hawai'i. Finally, in 1833, the idea became a reality. A Seamen's Bethel or House of God was established in Honolulu. The Society appointed Reverend John Diell as the first chaplain of the Bethel. Shortly after that, a Lahaina chapel was also begun.

Seamen's chapel, the Honolulu Bethel. SAMUEL CHENERY DAMON / WIKIMEDIA

The dedication of the Honolulu Bethel was held on Thursday, November 28, 1833, and was well-attended by the different segments of the community. Royalty was represented by Kamehameha III and his premier, Chiefess Kīnaʻu. Also, other high-born chiefs of the land were present. The foreign community of Honolulu had a good turnout. Shipmasters, their families, single seamen, and teachers and their pupils from the Oahu Charity School, a school which taught foreign and part-Hawaiian children to read and write English, were also there.

It was a first step for Reverend Diell, who also organized an Oahu Bethel Church which serviced the foreign community. Eventually, however, the work became too much for him and he exhausted himself in the service of ill and disabled seamen. At age thirty-three, he died of tuberculosis.

The new chaplain of the Honolulu Seamen's Bethel was a talented and energetic churchman by the name of Samuel Damon. Reverend Damon expanded further on the job of chaplain. In addition to religious and social duties, he began publishing *The Temperance Advocate* and *Seamen's Friend* which later was shortened to *The Friend,* and which was the first local newspaper to seriously devote its pages to the nautical community. It had articles on ships, whaling, marine news and statistics, as well as pieces on temperance and current curfew hours for Honolulu seamen.

The "forgotten men" now had a place within the community. They had their own church, hospital, libraries, books, and newspaper. And they had a friend in Reverend Damon as well. Sometimes, as many as fifty sailors would come for a Sunday visit, talking, and socializing at the study in Chaplain Lane. He was never too busy to talk to them.

The problem of ill and disabled seamen had long been a black mark on the communities of Honolulu and Lahaina. With the establishment of a U.S. Marine Hospital in 1838, the situation was somewhat improved. The hospital cared for the men, many of whom were deserters who would never return to their ships. But not every sailor was eligible for hospital care. Only native-born Americans or those with naturalization papers could be admitted. Foreigners were denied treatment. And American crews on whalers and merchant vessels were manned largely by foreigners.

If a sailor could not go to the hospital, then he was placed with a boarding housekeeper who was supposed to "nurse" him back to recovery. Unfortunately, many of the keepers were irresponsible to the point of neglect. And they were greedy. Often, the sick man's funds were depleted to the poverty point by excessive charges made for "nursing" and "lodging." One unlucky German sailor found that by the time he was able to move around and do for himself, he had no money and was well on his way to insolvency.

The care and disposition of sick men fell under the jurisdiction of the Consulates in the port of Honolulu and Lahaina. These officers had the power to either place the sick man in a hospital, boarding home, or if the situation were grave enough, furnish him passage home with funds appropriated from Congress for that purpose.

There were substantial doubts concerning the operations of the Consulate at Lahaina. In an editorial of September 1852, *The Friend* suggested that the Lahaina Consulate's figures for expenditures concerning sick seamen were suspiciously high: nearly twice those of the Honolulu Consulate and more than three times as high as similar offices in leading foreign seaports. Mischief was hinted but there was no authority to substantiate such a charge or even to do some checking. There would be none for quite a while—not at least until the Lahaina chaplain, who was presently en route, would arrive to take charge of things.

So, the social rehabilitation of the lot of the sailor was a slow process. But in March 1855, a large step was taken. The Hawaiian government generously donated land to be used for a Sailor's Home. Such a Home would admit sailors of all nationalities and would be the first really decent establishment where a seamen could board and eat his meals. The site of the Home was strategically chosen—it would be as close to the waterfront as possible and would be a buffer between the newly arrived seamen and the grogshops and brothels. It adjoined the Bethel Church and could accommodate about seventy-five beds.

Thus, from the single Bethel came a whole complex catering to the social and spiritual needs of seamen and foreign community in Honolulu. Four new churches eventually emerged, and the reading and recreation rooms so dear to the hearts of the younger men of the whaling fleet were the nucleus and base for the modern YMCA.

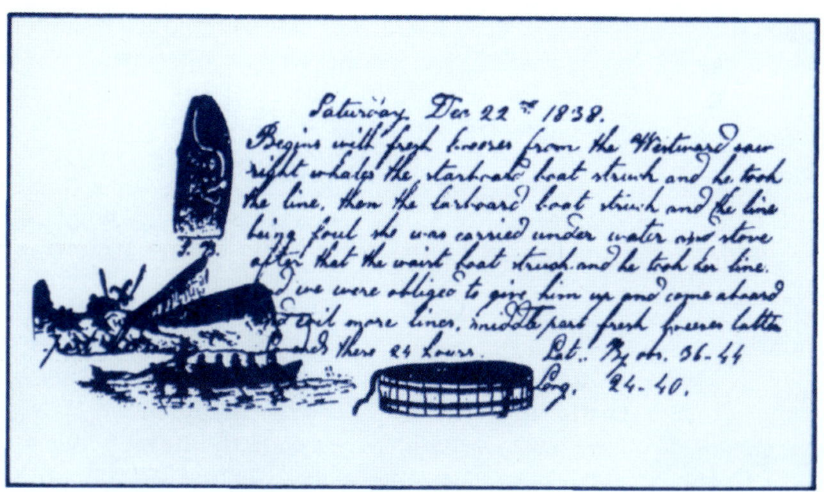

Saturday Dec 22nd 1838.
Begins with fresh breezes from the Westward saw
right whales the starboard boat struck and he took
the line, then the larboard boat struck and the line
being foul she was carried under water and stove
after that the waist boat struck and he took her line.
and we were obliged to give him up and come aboard
to [illegible] more lines, middle part fresh breezes latter
ends there 24 hours. Lat. By obs. 36-44
Long. 24-40.

THE DECLINE OF WHALING

The Islands began by having approximately sixty whaling vessels in 1822. Then, as new whaling grounds were uncovered in Northern Pacific waters, areas like Okhotsk, Bering, Anadir, and in the Arctic Ocean, the number gradually rose to over 140 annually. In 1846, it reached the astronomical figure of 596.

The peak years of whaling in Hawaiʻi were from 1840 to 1860. The industry started to decline with the discovery of petroleum in 1859 and the resulting drop in the price of whale oil. Other factors were the scarcity of whales and the amounting expenses of operating the industry. With costs steadily rising, provisioning and maintaining a ship for periods of three to four years at sea were being less and less justified by the smaller profits. And during the Civil War, the supply of ships had been badly depleted. A Confederate ship had set twenty-four whaleships ablaze, completely destroying them. And lastly, there were the two terrible freezes occurring in 1871 and in 1876. It was the 1871 freeze which gave the industry its gravest blow.

The 1871 Freeze
Disaster! Thirty-Three Ships Lost!

A document authored and signed by the masters of thirty-three whaling ships had been issued from Point Belcher, Arctic Ocean, and printed in the November 1, 1871 issue of *The Friend.* It describes the plight of the doomed vessels only too well:

> *...our ships cannot be got out this year, and there being no harbor that we can get our vessels into, and not having provisions enough to feed our crews to exceed three months, and being in a barren country where there is neither food or fuel to be obtained, we feel ourselves under the painful necessity of abandoning our vessels, and trying to work our way south with our boats, and if possible to get on board of ships that are south of the ice...*

The thirty-three ships were surrounded by ice. At the first storm they would be crippled by the massive shifts of ice trapping them. It was one of the most terrible disasters in whaling history. The masters were rugged whaling men who did not run from a little bad weather. Nevertheless, they had a healthy respect for the sea and were veterans of many storms. Assessing their situation, they realized their peril. Not only had they insufficient food or provisions but there was no sheltered harbor. The ships would be at the mercy of every heavy wind or gale. Under these circumstances, to stay would be suicide. They wrote the following:

> *...Should we be cast upon the beach it would be at least eleven months before we could look for assistance, and in all probability nine out of ten would die of starvation or scurvy before the opening of spring...*

Their solution was to take the small boats and head south. The whaling ships would have to be abandoned.

Opposite page: Whaling ships trapped in the Arctic Ocean.

The Whale Fishery "Laying On," 1852 by N. Currier. HAWAIʻI STATE ARCHIVES

On September 14, traveling south in their small boats with a minimum of clothing and provisions, the crewmen learned just how serious the situation really was. It was much worse than even the masters had imagined. Ice was all about them, a solid wall of glistening barrier, leaving only the narrowest strip of clear shoal water along the beach. This would be the case for the whole seventy miles south to Icy Cape. They struggled through the journey, camping at night on the beach under the arctic skies. On the 15th, they reached Icy Cape where a strong south wind and rough seas awaited them. It was all they could do to manage to reach the seven ships which were in deep waters, buffeted by the winds. Three of the seven ships (the *Arctic,* the *Midas,* and the *Progress*) each lost an anchor in an effort to get the travelers aboard. On the 16th, the last of the crew was safely aboard the ships. But now, the small

and sturdy boats which had rescued them from their icy prison would have to be sacrificed and cut adrift to flounder in the choppy gray waters. There was no room for them aboard the already over-crowded vessels.

The winds were still heavy when the ships at last weighed anchor, steering in a southwest direction toward Plover Bay and fresh provisions—enough to last them on the long journey back to Hawai'i.

The crew had come out of the catastrophe alive. It was the only bright spot in the picture. The losses on the abandoned ships were staggering. Only seven ships managed to come out of it and market their oil. In terms of the whaling industry, the loss was devastating. By the time the 1876 freeze occurred, this time with a loss of another twelve ships, the industry was in sharp decline.

EPILOGUE

The End of an Era

Whaling had been both good and bad for Hawai'i. On the good side, it had generated great monetary gain and economic growth for the Islands, as well as bringing the world to the small Island community. In the peak year of 1851, Honolulu had 558 whaleships and barks, 27 brigs, and 35 schooners—as well as 15,000 sailors. In that year alone, whaling more than paid its way as an industry to the Islands.

The evils, alas, had been widespread. Disease, drunkenness, lawlessness, and the disruption of a way of life. Attitudes and habits harmful to foreigners had proved equally detrimental to the Hawaiian and to the quality of life in the Islands.

Now, however, whaling was dying. A new day was dawning. Sugar, coffee, and cattle were taking over. Agriculture would replace whaling as the chief income producer for the Islands. On the Hawaiian horizon, the last few of the whaling ships continued to ply their trade, their numbers growing sparser with each day. Already, they were remnants of the past.

Whaling had passed, taking with it something lusty and romantic. The land had reclaimed its own, and the ports of Honolulu and Lahaina settled down to an agricultural era.

SUGGESTED READING

Alexander, Mary Charlotte. *The Story of Hawai'i.* New Haven: Yale University Press, 1941.

Bennett, Frederick D. *Narrative of a Whaling Voyage Round the Globe From the Year 1833-1836,* Vol. 1. New York: Da Capo Press, 1970.

Clemens, Samuel L. *Letters From Honolulu.* Honolulu: Thomas Nickerson, 1939.

Clemens, Samuel L. *Letters From the Sandwich Islands.* New York: Haskell House, 1972.

Dakin, W.J. *Whalemen Adventurers.* Sydney: Sirius Books, 1963.

Damon, Ethel M. *The Friend,* Vol. 103, June 1933, 124-31.

Gast, Ross H. *Don Francisco de Paula Marin, and Letters and Journal of Francisco de Paula Marin,* edited by Agnes Conrad. Honolulu: Hawaiian Historical Society, 1973.

Kuykendall, Ralph S. *The Hawaiian Kingdom,* Vol. I. Honolulu 1968.

Lawrence, Mary Chipman. *The Captain's Best Mate,* edited by Stanton Garner. Providence: Brown University Press, 1966.

Olmsted, Francis Allyn. *Incidents of a Whaling Voyage.* Tokyo: Chas. E. Tuttle, 1969.

Thrum, Thos. "When Sailors Ruled The Town," *Hawaiian Almanac & Annual* for 1921. Honolulu, December 1920.

Thurston, Mrs. L.G. *Life and times of Mrs. L.G. Thurston.* Honolulu: *The Friend,* 1934.

OTHER TITLES BY MAXINE MRANTZ

Women of Old Hawai'i

ISBN-13: 978-1-949307-35-1
© 2022, softcover, 6 × 9 in., 40 pages

Throughout the history of Hawai'i, women have played a crucial role in shaping the government, societal landscape, and future of the Islands by leading their people through immense change. *Women of Old Hawai'i* offers a basic overview of just a handful of the outstanding figures whose influence and work are still felt today.

Author Maxine Mrantz begins by just scratching the surface of what life was like for women in ancient Hawai'i, explaining the importance of genealogy and bloodlines, marriage and children, and women's roles as caregivers, artists, rulers, and lawmakers.

The Hawaiian Monarchy

ISBN-13: 978-1939487-94-0
© 2018, softcover, 6 × 9 in., 52 pages

Before Hawai'i was unified under a single monarch, its islands were ruled by warring chiefs. In 1810, the islands were finally united under a chief considered to be the greatest of Hawai'i's monarchs—Kamehameha the Great. His reign marked the beginning of the Kingdom of Hawai'i that lasted until its tragic overthrow in 1893 by American businessmen.

The Hawaiian Monarchy provides a narrative overview of each major monarch as they fought to protect Hawaiian sovereignty and its people, covering major events during their rule and the challenges they encountered.

Ka'iulani: Hawai'i's Tragic Princess

ISBN-13: 978-1939487-95-7
© 2018, softcover, 6 × 9 in., 40 pages

Ka'iulani's story spans the years when Hawai'i struggled against foreign domination, the monarchy was overthrown, and Hawai'i became a U.S. territory. It is a dramatic story, full of interest, beauty, and pathos, both fascinating as the biography of a singularly gifted, beautiful, and wise young woman, and valuable as a chapter in the history of the fiftieth state.

Richly illustrated with vintage photographs, *Ka'iulani: Hawai'i's Tragic Princess*, tells the story of Hawai'i's beloved princess while illuminating late nineteenth century Hawaiian history.

To order, visit www.mutualpublishing.com